RUN AND BE STILL

How I made it through the valley with my faith intact

ASHLEY CUNNINGHAM

WESTBOW
P R E S S
A DIVISION OF THOMAS NELSON

Scriptures taken from the Holy Bible, New International Version®, NIV®. Copyright ©
1973, 1978, 1984, 2011 by Biblica, Inc.™ Used by permission of Zondervan. All rights
reserved worldwide. www.zondervan.com The "NIV" and "New International Version" are
trademarks registered in the United States Patent and Trademark Office by Biblica, Inc.™

Scripture taken from the King James Version of the Bible.

Scripture taken from the New King James Version. Copyright 1979, 1980,
1982 by Thomas Nelson, inc. Used by permission. All rights reserved.

Scripture quotations taken from the Holy Bible, New Living Translation,
copyright 1996, 2004. Used by permission of Tyndale House
Publishers, Inc., Wheaton, Illinois 60189. All rights reserved

WestBow Press books may be ordered through booksellers or by contacting:

WestBow Press
A Division of Thomas Nelson
1663 Liberty Drive
Bloomington, IN 47403
www.westbowpress.com
1-(866) 928-1240

Because of the dynamic nature of the Internet, any web addresses or links contained in
this book may have changed since publication and may no longer be valid. The views
expressed in this work are solely those of the author and do not necessarily reflect the
views of the publisher, and the publisher hereby disclaims any responsibility for them.

Any people depicted in stock imagery provided by Thinkstock are models,
and such images are being used for illustrative purposes only.

Certain stock imagery © Thinkstock.

ISBN: 978-1-4908-0717-1 (sc)
ISBN: 978-1-4908-0718-8 (hc)
ISBN: 978-1-4908-0716-4 (e)

Library of Congress Control Number: 2013915824

Printed in the United States of America.

WestBow Press rev. date: 09/04/2013

For my husband, Phil, and my children, Tyler and Madison, my running partners and biggest cheerleaders. Thank you for not allowing me to take myself too seriously. Thank you for your support, for sharing me with this project, and for encouraging me to finish it. And for my sweet baby, Jay. Little one, thank you for reaching your tiny hands from heaven to draw me closer to God. I love you all so much!

Contents

Introduction

❦

This is what it is to be loved and to know that the promise was, when everything fell, we'd be held.

—Natalie Grant, "Held"

The following story is not mine, but God's. The words are not mine, but God's. I don't consider myself exceptional. Because we live in a broken world, pain and sorrow surround us each and every day. I know that there are others who have endured far greater hardships than I have. As followers of Christ, we are not immune to such hardships. But it is my belief that God allows us to suffer these things so that we may be a comfort to others, so that we may minister to others. Can someone who has never faced tragedy and loss even begin to comprehend the magnitude or enormity of the situation? Can someone who has never faced illness and an unknown future comprehend the fear and anxiety that ravage a body? Not only does God use our heartaches to teach us about His love and faithfulness, but when we reach the other side of our struggles, when we reach the mountain summit, when we can finally see the sun through the clouds, He gives us strength to offer words of comfort to others who find themselves in the middle of the storm we just weathered.

Praise be to the God and Father of our Lord Jesus Christ, the Father of compassion and the God of all comfort, who comforts us in all our troubles, so that we can comfort those in any trouble with the comfort we ourselves have received from God. (2 Cor. 1:3-4 NIV)

When you have the wisdom born of suffering, you are able to look around you and through that knowledge have your eyes opened to a mission field full of others who desperately need help. When you have "walked a mile in those shoes," you can say, "I get it, and I can do something about it to make it easier for the next person."

I hope that, through Christ, I am able to be a beacon of hope and a pillar of strength to anyone facing trials in their lives, facing a seemingly insurmountable obstacle. My words to you this day are to take comfort in the fact that God has you in the palm of His hand and He will not let you go, He will not let you down. Take heart: God has not forsaken you, and He has big plans for you.

"And the God of all grace, who called you to His eternal glory in Christ, after you have suffered a little while, will Himself restore you and make you strong, firm and steadfast" (1 Peter 5:10 NIV).

On the following pages, you will find my heart exposed so that I may share with you the lessons that I have learned. I pray that God will speak to you through my words so that they may be a blessing and comfort. This has been a labor of love ten years in the making. It has been a very personal journey for me, and I have continued to learn, discovering things about myself as well as learning how to experience Christ and turn to Him for all of my needs on a daily basis, not just in times of tragedy. I feel God is speaking to my heart, bidding me to "come." Just as in Matthew 14 when Jesus bade Peter to step out of the boat, I feel that He is bidding me to step out of all that I know is safe and in doing so, discover that through His power we are able to accomplish anything. With Christ we are able to achieve the impossible and walk on water. In this writing, I have thrown caution to the wind and abandoned myself to faith in Him, and Him alone.

Abraham Lincoln said, "I have been driven many times to my knees by the overwhelming conviction that I had nowhere to go. My own wisdom, and that of all about me, seemed insufficient for the day."

The Valley

⁓

Yea, though I walk through the valley of the shadow of death, I will fear no evil; for thou art with me; thy rod and thy staff they comfort me.

—Psalm 23:4 KJV

Even though I walk through the valley of the shadow of death,
Your perfect love is casting out fear
And even when I'm caught in the middle of the storms of this life
I won't turn back, I know you are near.

—Matt Redman, "You Never Let Go"

Down, down, down. I am free-falling into what feels like a bottomless pit. My arms and legs are flailing, my hands are grasping for something, *anything*, to grab hold of to stop my quick descent. I am spiraling out of control. The wind is rushing all around me, whistling in my ears. I am frantic. I am panicked. Then with a sickening thump, I hit. I lie motionless, my body broken and aching. All I can hear is my rapid, shallow breathing. My heart is racing, ready to beat out of my chest. My eyes strain to see what's around me, but it's so dark, so, so dark. The blackness that surrounds me is thick, almost tangible. It envelops me, surrounds me, swallows me whole. I scream, but it doesn't make a sound. This is the valley of the shadow of death, and I have suddenly found myself dropped right in the middle of it. The valley . . . deep. The valley . . . dark. The valley . . . dreadful.

Let's get real. Let go of pretenses; let go of the canned answers. Forget what you think I want to hear when I ask, "How are you?"

How many times do we plaster fake smiles on, swallow the lump in our throats, and lie through our teeth to people when they ask us that question? Today, for a second, be honest, at least with yourself, and answer that question. Grab a piece of paper and write down the answer if you need to. Drop the barrier between self and emotion and allow yourself to feel how you really are. Chances are, if you are reading this, your truthful answer is, "Not good." Do you know the valley? Are you free-falling out of control? Are you screaming, feeling stranded and desperately alone in the valley, searching the darkness for any trace of light? I am inviting you to continue to read my words; I am inviting you into my life. Let me make you a promise. I promise to be real with you. I promise to be authentic, genuine, and truthful. My words come from a fellow traveler, from a survivor of life's hurts—and oh, how life can hurt. As you continue reading and in exchange for the exposure of my soul, I ask something of you . . . honesty and an open mind. Be honest with yourself and release your heart to the healing that God offers; come to understand what it means to be held.

How many times have you complained to God about the way He is leading you? How many times have you asked God, "Why?"—a simple but extremely loaded question. Does it seem sometimes as if God waits until the last second to act or intercede and reveal His plan? If He isn't asking us to walk completely by faith, as if following Him down an unlit path literally through the valley of the shadow of death, we find our path only bright enough for the next step we have to take. We want to be able to plan ahead, or to at least have some semblance of control. We desire clear vision. Instead, our journey through the darkness makes us feel unnervingly vulnerable.

* * *

"The beginning of anxiety is the end of faith, and the beginning of true faith is the end of anxiety" (George Mueller).

"Faith is the confidence that what we hope for will actually happen; it gives us assurance about things we cannot see" (Heb. 11:1 NLT).

How did I come to my walk of faith? I can tell you one thing for sure: it didn't come easy. There have been many times I have found myself crying out in fear, hurt, and desperation from the darkness of the depths of the valley. But truly, truly I say to you, that which doesn't kill us only makes us stronger. Let me share my journey through life, so you can better understand what I am talking about. I have seen God's hand at work in all of the hardships and trials I have endured, and my faith has blossomed and come to life through the Holy Spirit at work within me.

Reflecting on my life, I am reminded of an amusement park ride. Not a roller coaster, although there have been plenty of ups and downs, but the old-fashioned cars. I am sure you know the ones. You drive your car along the path, and when your car gets too far to one side or the other, you hit the center guide bar and are forced to bring it back to the middle of the road. Depending on your speed, you may get a gentle bump to remind you to get back on course; or if you're going faster, you end up with something closer to whiplash. I have experienced both.

So, who am I? I am by nature a planner, a list maker, a controller, and a worrier. I am the type of person who will do others' work for them so that I know it's done correctly—and by correctly, I mean my way. I am sure there are many of you out there nodding your head in agreement. We know who we are. The responsibilities that we carry are sometimes crushing, but we wouldn't have it any other way. There is something about being able to check items off a list that makes us feel fulfilled. I also know that there is another group of you shaking your head because we, in all of our planning and list making and worrying, drive you crazy. So, because of my planning, list making, and white-knuckle controlling, when it came to my life, I of course had a plan.

I went to college and got a degree, check. I married my high school sweetheart, check. We bought a house and started a family, check. Everything according to my plan. I had a career that afforded me the opportunity to work from home, a beautiful eighteen-month-old son, and we were expecting our second child, another baby boy. Life was rolling along nicely, but I was getting awfully close to bumping that guide bar.

About a week after a routine sonogram, I got a call from my doctor that set in motion my valley descent. Upon further review of the sonogram by the radiologist, an umbilical cord cyst was discovered. We had to schedule an appointment to see a neonatal specialist. I was terrified; this knocked my feet out from underneath me because this was definitely *not* part of my plan. Surely, with some prayer, God would take care of this.

Control is a funny thing. We seek to maintain control in an effort to combat fear. Control is, in essence, a defensive strategy to keep from going down an undesired or unknown path. This was a pretty astute description of me. In the past, one way that I had been able to battle the fear of the unknown was through gaining knowledge; in knowledge, I had control. So I researched umbilical cord cysts. What I found out was that most dissipated by the thirtieth week, and one of the greatest threats they posed was Down syndrome. Okay, so we might have to adjust the plan somewhat.

After meeting with the neonatologist, we found out that he felt our chances for Down syndrome were not any more elevated than had there been no cyst. The actual cyst was about one inch in diameter, and as far as he could see, not hampering the blood flow to the fetus at all. He wanted to see us at thirty weeks. Translation: plan back on track.

We prayed that the cyst would dissipate but had been reassured that if not, the possibility of complications was slim. Summer came and went. We decided to sell our home, as we had simply outgrown it, especially with another baby on the way. My goal was to be in our new house by the time the baby was born. Are you sensing the theme here that this was all about me? Unfortunately, that is not the way we are called to live our lives.

At my thirty-week checkup with the specialist, another sonogram was performed, revealing that our baby was rather small compared to what was considered normal. In fact, he was only in the twenty-fifth percentile for length and weight. My doctor put me on a special diet, trying to jump-start our baby's growth. We also developed a labor and delivery plan, as the time was drawing near. The cyst was still there, and again he assured me that things seemed okay. Things weren't as okay as everyone thought.

Tuesday, October 16, prepare for whiplash. You never know when your feet hit the floor in the morning what will transpire before the day's end. As I sat in the rocking chair in the early morning light, I realized that I had not felt the baby move at all yet. Being that he was a very active baby, especially in the morning, I decided to drink some orange juice, thinking that might get him moving. But to no avail. My husband suggested calling the doctor's office, just so that I wouldn't worry needlessly—or so we thought. They asked me to come in right away, and the little voice in the back of my head that had already been suggesting the worst began getting a little louder.

Still not having felt the baby move, I was trying to reason with the growing fear that was threatening to take over. Somewhere in the back of my mind, though, I already knew that he was gone. Call it a mother's intuition, but my conscious mind was not able to accept that yet.

After I arrived at the doctor's office and was escorted directly into an examining room, my doctor began looking for the baby's heartbeat. Immediately a heartbeat was heard and a look of relief came over my husband's face, but I knew that it didn't sound right. My thoughts were confirmed when the doctor took my pulse, simultaneously matching the sound of the racing heart we heard with my own heartbeat.

At that point, the panic I was feeling was threatening to choke me, and she suggested a sonogram. It didn't take long for her to confirm what we all already knew but were afraid to voice. There was no heartbeat—and in that instant, I felt a loss greater than I have ever known. My life was forever changed. The overwhelming sense of helplessness pervaded every ounce of my being. To be a person who is such a "doer" and never have the chance to *do* something to fix it, never have a chance to save my unborn son—I couldn't grasp the reality and finality in that. He was taken from me, from my body, without my knowing. I had failed. I had failed my baby, myself, and my family. I never had the chance to mother him. He never had a chance to be my son. Our family was broken, and I was decimated.

Everything that happened after that was a formality; our son was already gone. I was on autopilot, and the awful task of telling our families became my husband's. Our doctor suggested going home, dealing with the shock, and then coming back in the next day for the worst part, labor and delivery. That evening we surrounded ourselves with family and began thinking about things that parents never think that they will have to deal with: funeral arrangements for our infant son.

All I could think about was how was I going to be able to do this? Would I want to see him? Would I be able to hold him, or would it be too hard? What was I going to do with the outfit that I had bought to bring him home in? He never was coming home. What I realized later was that he was already home.

The next evening we arrived at the hospital and had to register; I can remember hoping that no one would ask too many questions. The lady at the registrar's desk, however, simply made mention that, "Wow, you don't look very big to be having a baby." I can't remember what I answered her, but I do remember thinking that this was surely the first of many uncomfortable conversations in the days to come. People don't know what to say; I never did. Here is what I learned. The people who show up for you do so because they love you and they are trying to help you and comfort you in the only way they know how. In Ed Underwood's book *When God Breaks Your Heart*, he writes, "So many Christians tell me that they don't know what to say. Then they open their mouths and prove it." I know that to ask a hurting person to also be the bigger person and see past the hurtful words to the loving intent that is behind them is like adding salt to a wound. Nobody ever really knows what to say or do, but at least they have the courage to show up and try. Have you found yourself on the receiving end of these hurtful words? I would remind you of this: these people have shown up, they have *volunteered* to stand beside you, hold your hand, cry with you, or pray with you, not because they understand it—tragedy doesn't make sense. They may feel inadequate and uncomfortable, but they have shown up because *they love you*; and while it may not remove all your hurt and frustration over the way they show it, I hope that with a shift in thinking, it may remove the sting at least a little bit.

At thirty-two weeks into my pregnancy, after seven hours of labor, our son, Jay Brady Cunningham, was born at 3:12 a.m., weighing three pounds, five ounces, and 17 ¾ inches long. He was a perfect little boy, with ten long fingers and ten beautiful little toes. He looked as if he were sleeping, and I kept waiting for his eyes to flutter open. When they brought him to me, he looked like a little baby doll, dressed in the tiniest clothing that I have ever seen.

However, reality really hit when after a loud crash, he never stirred. My husband said his immediate thought was, "Shh, the baby." This was going to be quite an adjustment for all of us.

How were we going to explain to our son, whom we had been preparing for a brother, that there was going to be no brother? Luckily, he only asked once where our baby went, and I simply told him the truth . . . he was with Jesus. Thankfully, that seemed to satisfy him.

My mother, mother-in-law, and husband were all there to see Jay, and we all got a chance to hold him. I held my baby for as long as they would let me, and eventually just after dawn, someone came to take him away. That was the last time I saw my infant son.

It wasn't until a few days later that I realized that I never sang to him, something I did quite frequently with my older son, and that tore me apart I think more than anything. If there is one thing that I wish I could go back and do, that is it. Regret is an extremely powerful emotion. It added to the already helpless, out-of-control feelings that I was struggling through. I learned that there are some things that you will never be able to right, and regret is a very heavy burden to shoulder.

A pastor who is a wonderful friend to my husband and me performed the private funeral service. I thought that I had prepared myself for this and that the worst part was surely behind me. That was until I saw the tiniest casket I have ever seen in my life. There are just some things that never should be, and this is one of them. During the short service, our pastor spoke about how God could empathize with us because he too lost a Son. God sent His Son to this earth to suffer persecution and a death in a most horrible fashion so that we might have eternal life. With Jesus' death, all of our sins were washed away; and if we accept this gift of forgiveness, we will have a home in heaven for eternity. The pastor said that God must have thought our son was very special, for he was taken home without ever having to feel pain, disappointment, or persecution. That was a huge revelation to me, and that thought has comforted me many times as I play the what-if game.

I never thought that this would happen to me. No one does. You don't have pain, loss, and suffering on your list to check off. I kept thinking if I could just wake up, this would all be a dream. Things seemed surreal, like sometimes they were in slow motion and sometimes they were on fast-forward. I found myself in the middle of the valley, shrouded in darkness, my entire being aching from the force of the impact of the fall. What is your valley? Have you had such an unspeakable pain in your life that you thought you couldn't go on? I was left sprawled out on the valley floor, hurt and crying. But God was there, and He picked me up and lovingly tended to my hurts; He pleaded with me not to do this on my own. My car, which had been veering off track, had hit the guide bar.

> Seek God in your darkness and He will be your light.
> Seek God in your questions and He will be your
> answer.
> Seek God in your anger and He will be your peace.
> Seek God in your sorrow and He will be your
> comforter.
> Seek God in your uncertainty and He will be your
> confidence.

Seek God in your sin and He will be your redeemer.
Seek God in your forgiveness and He will be your
    salvation.
Seek God in your salvation and He will be your
    eternity.

(Kathe Wunnenberg)

My husband and I had both grown up in church, he Catholic and myself in a large fundamental Christian church, so we both had strong religious backgrounds and were really good at "being Christian," but it wasn't until this moment in time that I really learned what faith was all about, for without it I would have fallen to pieces. Faith is not an insurance policy against pain and suffering, but an assurance that God will be with us, no matter what.

I can't say at what moment it happened, but after hearing that our son was gone, faith took over and God became my source of strength. Suddenly I had a sense of peace. Yes, I was hurting badly, but I had to believe that God was good and had a plan, and though I might never know the reason, surely there was one. I also knew that God's heart was breaking with mine.

You may be saying, "Great for you, but I am not there." So let me stop for a moment here and tell you that not every day was good. It wasn't as if there were some magical prayer that made it all go away. I was hurting! I had lost a child and I had bad days, but I have found that we have to choose our attitude. We have to choose to see beyond where we are right now, even though that anger and bitterness and sadness sometimes feel so justified. Every day that we choose God over our anger, it gets easier and easier to continue making that choice. Right now your bad days may be outnumbering your good days, but please don't stop here. Don't get snared in the valley. Josh Wilson sings a wonderful song, "Savior, Please," that has ministered to my heart so many times as I have found myself trying so hard to just "buck up" and be tough, but we will never, never be able to do it on our own. A portion of the chorus says this: "I try to be so tough, but I'm just not strong enough. I can't do this alone, God. I need you to hold on to me." If you aren't there yet, it's okay; it will take time, but before you go on, take a moment and just ask God to hold on to you, and see where it goes from there. He would love to if you will you let Him.

*   *   *

A few years later, one night close to Halloween, my five-year-old son and I decided to take a "spooky" four-wheeler ride though the "haunted" woods. He was snuggled up on my lap with just a flashlight to light the woods around us. Venturing deeper into the woods, he became more and more frightened. The flashlight's beam could only illuminate small slices of all that was around us, leaving much to the imagination. For him it was exhilarating and terrifying at the same time, and as much as he wanted it to end, he also loved it. As I thought about that night ride, I came to understand that the darkness that surrounds us, and terrified my son, is much like the larger journey that we are all on. Here on earth, we fear many enemies—some imagined, and others real. We lock our doors and turn on alarms. My son hoped that something wouldn't jump out of the darkness from beyond our path. Isn't that the same fear that all of us have? Having to face those unexpected events that spring out of the darkness and catch us totally unprepared? Don't we struggle with putting one foot in front of the other when we can't see the path, when we are only able to see the "small slices" as we try to move forward? David Jeremiah said, "The purpose of the places in which we lose our vision is to strengthen our faith." This truly is what it means to walk by faith, and although we desperately long for God to shine a floodlight on the path so that we are able to see the entirety of His plan, if He did, what use would there be for faith? Faith would have no reason to exist, for faith is needed for what we *can't* see and *can't* touch. Faith is what we use to battle the creatures, those life-altering events, that we fear are hiding just beyond our vision in the dark.

"For we walk by faith, not by sight." (2 Cor. 5:7 NIV)

The Bible is filled with examples of those who have walked by faith. Faith is not just a nice warm feeling that God gives us. Faith is an attitude; it equals action. Faith is stepping out in obedience to what God calls us toward. Walking by faith is God's plan, and He blesses us when we obey His plans, not ours. Can you imagine the fear that filled the Israelites as they took their first steps into the Red Sea with towering walls of water on either side of them? The amount of faith that it took as they continued in farther and farther, realizing that there was no way out? Pharaoh was behind them, and the sea surrounded them. All they could do was put one foot in front of the other and continue moving forward. Or what about Noah, who was instructed to build an ark? Can you imagine the looks he got as he began this massive construction project? He had been warned of "things not yet seen," which was very simply rain, as God's judgment was coming in the form of a great flood. Rather than question God, he picked up his hammer while the sun was still shining and got to work. His faith silenced all the rational objections. Can you imagine the jeering and ridicule, not to mention danger, the Israelites faced as they marched around the walls of Jericho for seven days straight? God's method for defeating the enemy was anything but traditional. They marched and trumpeted and marched some more, and on the seventh day, with a mighty yell, God's power tumbled the walls.

To escape the darkness of the valley, we must take action. Just like every one of these faithful servants, we have to step out in faith into the unknown, even when it hurts or is scary to do so, even when your world is falling down around you like the walls of Jericho. In God, we have a lighted path to follow, and it is in that light that we will find safety and comfort. While we may fear what is just beyond the light, lurking in the darkness, ready to pounce on us given the chance, we cannot allow it to rule our lives and control our walks. We must live our lives with complete faith in Christ, just as my son had in me, flashlight in hand, on our ride through the dark woods. At the end of the day, our Father is protecting us, and although it may be scary, He is holding the flashlight, and we can take comfort in that. When your hope is in God rather than the things you desire from Him, you no longer need to fear the darkness. This is how, strangely, the unknown can become powerless over us, how one footstep after another, we can find victory while walking in the dark.

*We do this by keeping our eyes on Jesus, the champion who
initiates and perfects our faith. Because of the joy awaiting
Him, He endured the cross, disregarding its shame. Now
He is seated in the place of honor beside God's throne.
(Heb. 12:2 NLT)*

God didn't promise an easy path. Sometimes we assume
because we are followers of Christ, we should be protected and
have an easy road to travel. That is not the case. In fact, Jesus tells
us in John 16:33 to expect trouble. "I have told you all this so that
you may have peace in me. Here on earth you will have many trials
and sorrows. But take heart, because I have overcome the world." It
is in our times of trial that we are able to experience real spiritual
growth and godlike character, and that we are truly able to feel the
hand of God holding us close and comforting us. After all, while
the mountaintops provide a beautiful view, the valleys are where
the lush grass and flowers grow. I haven't come easily to this walk
by faith. The pathway has been so dark that I wondered if it were
safe to continue on. Are you there? Is one foot in front of the other
the way you get through every day? The amount of growth you will
achieve depends on your response to whatever it is that is standing
directly in the path.

We will all face a day when everything that we thought we
knew falls apart, when we are suddenly thrust into the darkness,
stumbling and fumbling. The question is, how do you handle it?
Where do you turn? Do you let your Father pick you up and tend
your wounds, or do you turn to worldly "problem solvers," who
will only offer a temporary release from pain and fear? We need a

belief system that can withstand the pressure, pain, and criticism that life is sure to bring. We need to be able to stand firm on the Rock of the Ages, look life square in the eye, and say, "Bring it!" and be ready to behold the power of the almighty God. If we don't, we will surely falter in the darkness.

Fast-forward ten years, and you will find me busy. Busy, busy, busy. I can remember joking in August of that year that if anyone needed me, my next availability was in February. I was busy raising a family, busy being a wife, busy managing my own business, playing bus driver between school, sporting events, practices, and friends, volunteering in the junior high youth group at church . . . The list goes on and on, but if you have ever watched a hamster running in its wheel, that was exactly how I felt. Running and running and not getting anywhere. There were not enough hours in the day, let alone the week, to accomplish everything that I kept piling onto my plate. Barbara Stanny, a speaker and life coach, has said, "Ask us to lighten our load, actually say no to a task, and we start to panic. As if our world would shatter if we slowed down. The truth is, we've become so controlled by shoulds, oughts, musts, have-tos that we've lost sight of what's honestly important." I was so there.

> You would think only so much can go wrong
> Calamity only strikes once
> And you assume this one has suffered her share
> Life will be kinder from here.
> (Natalie Grant, "Our Hope Endures")

You know what they say about assumptions . . .

The week before Thanksgiving, I started having heart palpitations. Is it any wonder with the pace that I was keeping? This wasn't entirely uncommon for me, and because of this I already had an echocardiogram scheduled. What was uncommon was that this time they didn't go away. Three days after the palpitations started, I had my echo. The tech who did my echo informed me I had an irregular heartbeat, but because of a family emergency and the upcoming holiday, my films wouldn't be read for seven to ten days. I had convinced myself that what I was feeling was in my head, so this confirmation and new information caused me to panic. Was there something I should be doing, something I shouldn't be doing? I made a call to a cousin who is a cardiac nurse.

Within an hour, I had been squeezed into an amazing cardiologist's schedule; he also found what he believed to be a heart murmur and some abnormal noises in my carotid arteries. A twenty-four-hour Holter test was ordered and revealed that I had over three thousand irregular beats in that period. After a couple of days and numerous phone calls, my new doctor was finally able to get a copy of my echo, and thankfully everything looked normal. But I was still having palpitations, and he still heard the unusual noise in my neck. I was only thirty-three. My blood work was all normal. I was healthy—or so we thought—so none of this was adding up.

The week before Christmas, more tests were ordered. This time a stress echo and a carotid ultrasound. The morning after these tests were completed, I got a call from my doctor. Have you ever been on the receiving end of a phone call that seems to make time stop? When the doctor called to inform us of the umbilical cord cyst, it was a scorching hot summer day; we had been swimming, and when my cell phone rang, I was standing in the kitchen at my grandma's house. This time I got hit with my news as I was passing through the dining room and snatched the ringing phone while frantically getting our house ready for Christmas dinner with our extended family. I found myself sinking into one of the dining room chairs as he spoke.

The carotid ultrasound showed some unusual findings, a narrowing of the carotid arteries. He began talking about medical conditions that I had never heard of and a need for specialized doctors. He also told me they wanted to do an MRI of my chest, abdomen, neck, and brain as soon as possible. Now we were starting to talk about some pretty serious stuff. He said that I shouldn't need to go to the ER unless I was having really bad headaches. That news itself was enough to cause a really bad headache! My mind was spinning, and my heart was racing irregularly. I was on a blood pressure medication that was sapping all of my energy, but I plastered on a smile and kept up the festive mood for my family. The week between Christmas and New Year's, I spent two hours in an MRI machine. Two days after my MRI, I woke up and realized that my heart was back in rhythm, and it has been in rhythm ever since (more on that later.)

We followed up with my cardiologist that next week. He came into the room and said without any hesitation, "The MRI showed some very significant narrowing of some very major arteries. I don't understand it, and I am going to recommend that you see a vascular specialist." *What!* So far, every test had resulted in more questions and no answers. Now that we finally had something, I was completely unprepared for what it was. For the last six weeks, we had been searching for answers, never believing it would be anything as life-changing as it was. In short, what the MRI revealed was that the major arteries that supplied the blood to my arms were both narrowed: the left artery was completely closed, the right one was 60 percent narrowed, and my carotid arteries were between 30 and 50 percent narrowed. That was a lot of news to process, especially since I wasn't having any major symptoms. Did my arms get tired? Well sure, but I figured I was out of shape. Did I have headaches? Yes, but not debilitating. I blamed it on the weather or allergies. The doctor stepped out to make a phone call to a specialist at the Cleveland Clinic whom he had done his fellowship with. He came back with an appointment for me in three days. This vascular specialist had taken my doctor's call in the middle of a procedure and was getting ready to leave the country for a couple of weeks, but agreed to see me on the morning that he was leaving. God's hand had been in this from the beginning.

Three days later, we made the hour-and-fifteen-minute drive to downtown Cleveland through rush-hour traffic, thankful to live so close to a world-class medical facility. After a thorough visit and another round of ultrasounds, this vascular specialist made the determination that what they were seeing was in fact inflammation. This had been the "best guess" diagnosis up to this point, but because all of my blood work continued to come back normal, it hadn't been verified. While we were there, he referred me to another doctor within the Rheumatologic and Immunologic Institute. At this point, they were pretty sure it was an autoimmune disease, but which one, no one would, or could, say, so I was left to continue my research and guesses. Fear and knowledge and control, an endless cycle that I was becoming very familiar with. Let me say, while there is a wealth of information available to us today, the Internet can be a very dangerous place when we begin to play doctor and self-diagnosis.

Another week and another trip to downtown Cleveland and the Cleveland Clinic. This time we came home with a diagnosis, an answer, and heavy hearts. I was diagnosed with Takayasu's arteritus, an extremely rare autoimmune disease that in the United States only affects two people (mostly women between age fifteen to thirty-five) per million. My immune system was attacking my arteries, causing inflammation, which was in turn damaging these blood vessels. The vessels most commonly affected are the branches of the aorta that supply blood to the arms and travel through the neck to provide blood to the brain. The aorta itself is also often affected. Basically, I am at war with myself. My body is attacking my main arteries as if they were an infection. In addition, we learned that similar to cancer, Takayasu's arteritus can go into remission and then for some undetermined reason flare back up. Unfortunately, this disease is swathed in the unknown. Doctors aren't sure how to tell if the treatment is working; MRIs can show narrowing of my arteries, but the doctors can't be sure if it is from inflammation or from damage. Blood tests can come back completely normal, but you can still have inflamed tissue. Even the very symptoms that would indicate that the disease is active can be silent.

So, how do they treat this mysterious illness? In the absence of information, my doctor began treating me as if I were in an active phase of Takayasu's arteritus. I was started on mega doses of steroids in an effort to corral my immune system, in essence shutting it down. As long as I am not in "attack mode," the inflammation will stay at bay. I was instructed that every day for the rest of my life, I need to be taking my blood pressure, as that will be one of the earliest indicators that the disease is flaring up or spreading. I also need monthly blood tests and have to be closely monitored by a cardiologist. (My arteries are already narrowed and compromised, so any amount of heart disease in the future could cause major issues.) Another major complication with this disease is obviously something as simple as a common cold. Because my system is compromised, any cough, fever, and so on needs to be addressed immediately before it can gain a major foothold.

Before our appointment was over, I asked about the connection between Takayasu's arteritus and the heart palpitations that set this whole journey in motion. The amazing thing that I learned was that there wasn't a connection between the two. The problems I was having with my heart were electrical. Looking back, it doesn't take much of a leap of faith to see that God was short-circuiting my heart, causing symptoms that continued until the "right" test was ordered, the MRIs showing the inflammation. After which, the heart condition went away. Without these tests and a doctor who wasn't content to just accept the palpitations as an anomaly, who knows how long this disease would have gone undetected and untreated?

The major piece of information that I took away from our appointment was this: only 3 percent of those diagnosed die within the first five years. *What!* You have got to be kidding me. Three percent may not sound that bad, but when there are so few people with the disease, I didn't like those odds. I was physically sick that evening, but put on a smile so that my kids, ages nine and twelve, couldn't see what was going on.

Once again, I never thought that this would happen to me. Calamity only strikes once, right? *Desperate* had a new meaning, and as I cried that night trying to come to grips with everything that I had learned, I kept thinking that I wasn't afraid of dying; I knew where I was going. But what absolutely killed me, what broke my heart, was the thought of leaving my children and husband to deal with life without "Mom," the thought of them having to watch me suffer through this illness, helpless to do anything. There was no cure. There was no "take these pills, and you will be fine." Here was my old friend helplessness again, and he brought with him desperation. This was a forever kind of thing, but who knew how long that would be and what that was going to look like in the meantime. Was this going to be what killed me? The grief and unrest came in wave upon wave. I had walked out of the doctor's office straight off a cliff and was plummeting out of control again into the valley, swathed deeply in the blackness. And this is where God again stepped in and picked up the pieces.

The next morning my husband sent me a text message that said I needed to listen to a song, "God Is Still God" by Heather Williams. As soon as he got in the car that morning headed to work, it came on the radio. I immediately downloaded it but waited to listen to it until I was on my way home after dropping the kids at school. As I listened to it, the tears started again, and I began to let go of everything that I had been carrying since all of the testing started. This is where the wheels of my out-of-control, careening car quite literally caught on that strong guide bar, and the wild swerving stopped.

The song, which took my breath away, could have been pulled directly from my heart that day. Heather Williams, in her own words, says this about the song's message. "It's a song that speaks so clearly into an insecurity that we can get when life just comes at us at full speed. It's very easy to try to take control of it ourselves. To let God take control of things is freeing, but it can also be scary at times. I also love that this song is a conversation with somebody. Sometimes we feel like we have to have the right things to say, but if we just offer them the comfort that God is still in control, that in and of itself can be a powerful statement. I like the simplicity of the message." And this was where I found myself that morning.

> Where our hope is spent and our faith don't work
> But nothing lasts forever
> The only thing that matters
> Is God is still God and He holds it together.
> Heather Williams, "God is Still God"

The next song that came on my iPod was "Blessings," by Laura Story. The theme behind this song is that sometimes our greatest blessings come through our suffering. I knew in that moment that God was speaking to me that morning through the music on my iPod. He was my DJ, and I pulled the car over and began to pray.

Because of the nature of this disease, life was never going to go back to being "normal" again. I call this my "life interrupted."

It is my new normal, or maybe abnormal. Every day when I wake up, I have to take my blood pressure because that will be one of the earliest signs that my disease has become active again and is spreading. So every day I pray that my blood pressure remains the same as it was yesterday, that my disease remains in remission. Every day I take medication that is designed to shut my immune system down and keep the Takayasu's arteritis at bay, so I pray that I stay healthy, that my family stays healthy, because something as minor as a common cold could send me to the hospital and wreak havoc with an already compromised immune system. I pray that the side effects of the medication that is supposed to be making me well, will go away—the headaches, the ravenous appetite, the shaking hands and jittery nerves that assault me every day. Every day I am reminded that I am sick, even though I may not look like it, even though I may not feel like it.

This disease continues to hang over my head. There is a false sense of security that lies just around the bend, taunting me as the days pass and the tests come back normal. But all it takes is one blip on a blood test that requires a retest or a splitting headache that seems to be without cause to shake me to my very core and remind me just how slippery the slope is that I am perched on. Seven months after being diagnosed, while we were on a family vacation, I had a major scare. My vision became compromised to the point that I felt like I was trying to see through someone else's glasses. I couldn't judge distance and became lethargic and achy. Fear coursed through my veins like ice as I wondered what was going on. It came on suddenly and without warning. What I found out after teleconferencing with my doctor was that I was experiencing withdrawal symptoms. My body's adrenal glands had gone into hibernation and were having a hard time waking up to supplement the necessary cortisol that was no longer being provided medicinally. Every time an incident like this occurs, I am reminded that I am sick, that I am not in control, and larger than that, there is not a thing I can do about it. I am constantly pushing this terror back down, beating it down as you would rising bread dough. No matter how many times you push it down, it eventually rises back up.

And because of all of this, every day, I am utterly dependent on God. He has placed Himself squarely in the path of my new normal, and every day I remember exactly who He is and who I am. He is God, and I am not.

I began feeling a little bit like a crazy person running around proclaiming God's greatness in the middle of the storm I was weathering, but I just couldn't help myself. I felt certain that God would use this disease for His glory. I was hungry for the Word of God unlike I ever had been before and began writing again. It was something I hadn't done for years and had missed so desperately. After losing our son, I had felt compelled to reach out in compassion to others who are hurting, but I wasn't sure how and life just kept getting in the way. It wasn't until now that I felt God saying, "Okay, now, go!" I hit the ground running and haven't looked back. The incessant tick, tick, tick of our time here on earth is louder than ever before, and I don't intend to waste a second of it.

So, there it is, all laid out, my life. Grief, fear, pain, worry, anger, confusion, regret—the list goes on. Insert your struggle in the blank. I have been there, and implore you to understand that there isn't anyone more powerful, there isn't anyone more equipped to take all of it away than God. We cannot do this on our own, and more important than that, we will fail every time we try. Without that center bar guiding us along, our car would be haphazardly veering right and left, leaving the path, getting stuck, and ultimately crashing.

The valley . . . deep. The valley . . . dark. The valley . . . dreadful. In my journey, through all of my bumps, bruises, and scrapes as I have fallen, I have learned some lessons that are not just important, but essential, to remember in our struggles. When you find yourself thrust into life's valleys, remember Psalm 23:4: "Yea, though I walk through the valley of the shadow of death, I will fear no evil; for thou art with me; thy rod and thy staff they comfort me" (Ps. 23:4 KJV). *Thou art with me . . .* First, you are not alone; everyone experiences trials in their lives, and when those times come, God is upholding you. Secondly, our suffering has a purpose in God's plan and is controlled by God. *Thy rod and thy staff they comfort me . . .* God will provide the grace for endurance, and our weakness will be made perfect in His strength. Finally, we must surrender ourselves totally. This happens when we stop wrestling with the will of God and start walking in it, no matter how steep or dark or deserted the path may seem. If we miss even one of these principles, if we take our eyes off of God for a second and focus on our problems, we will surely falter and collapse under the weight of our struggles. God intends for our struggles to prepare us for greater things. We have to accept them as such and allow God to work in us and through us. Charles Stanley put it this way: "If we don't respond the right way to hardships, we will get the valley treatment without the glory."

Independently, these all are extensive topics. There are entire books devoted to them individually. The following pages examine each of these principles in terms of "the big picture" and what they mean to us in very practical, everyday ways. I share their lessons, learned through the eyes of a sufferer.

Though I walk through . . . come walk with me, walk with God, and let's get *through* this valley, no matter how persistently the shadows lap at our heals. Let's walk together toward victory, peace, and rest in Christ.

Jesus Loves You

⤸

31

I pray that from His glorious, unlimited resources He will empower you with inner strength through His Spirit. Then Christ will make His home in your hearts as you trust Him. Your roots will grow down into God's love and keep you strong. And may you have the power to understand, as all God's people should, how wide, how long, how high, and how deep His love is. May you experience the love of Christ, though it is too great to understand fully.

—Ephesians 3:16-19 NLT

We have sung the song since we were little kids: "Jesus loves me this I know, for the Bible tells me so." The Bible is full of verses about God's love for us. Perhaps the most often-quoted verse of the Bible is this one: "For God loved the world so much that He gave His one and only Son, so that everyone who believes in Him will not perish but have eternal life" (John 3:16 NLT). Watch any major sporting event on TV and someone will be holding up a poster with John 3:16 on it; players wear it on their eye blacks. But because it's everywhere and we memorize it as small children, I think it sometimes loses its effect on us. It becomes just a few words strung together without meaning.

Before we can go any further, we have to fully understand the most basic principle that all of the others will be built off of. Love. Not love as you and I know it, but God's love. This love is unfathomable; it extends beyond the bounds of our finite comprehension. My prayer is the same for you as Paul's, written above to the church at Ephesus. That you become empowered with inner strength, that your roots will grow down into God's love and that you will understand how wide, long, high, and deep God's love is for you. If we are unable to understand this, if we are unable to accept this, then we can go no further in our journey toward glory because everything else that I will share with you is based off this one truth. This is the firm foundation that everything else is built upon.

When you are tempted to doubt the overwhelming love that God pours out to you, when you find yourself thinking, "God loves everyone, but I am just one of billions, and by the time God's love reaches me it has to be spread pretty thin" or "There are much bigger problems in the world; why would God want to focus His affection on me?" remember these verses:

> And I am convinced that nothing can ever separate us from God's love. Neither death nor life, neither angels nor demons, neither our fears for today nor our worries about tomorrow—not even the powers of hell can separate us from God's love. No power in the sky above or in the earth below—indeed, nothing in all creation will ever be able to separate us from the love of God that is revealed in Christ Jesus our Lord. (Rom. 8:38-39 NLT)

There is nothing you can do to make God love you more. And there is nothing you can do to make God love you less. Love is not something God does. It is who He is.

Since my diagnosis, I have felt God's love overwhelmingly. Does that mean that it wasn't there before? No. God had been waiting to shower me with love, but I was too busy to take the time to accept it. Crazy, but oh so true. Life has a tendency to get in the way, but God has the capability to slam on the brakes and make you take a pit stop and take notice of Him.

God's love came into focus very clearly for me on Easter Sunday three months after having been diagnosed with Takayasu's arteritis, as we stood in church singing "I Stand Amazed." Written in 1905 by Charles Gabriel, it is a timeless hymn, as true today as the day it was written. As we got to the second verse, the tears started rolling down my cheeks uncontrollably and continue to do so to this day every time I hear this song. Why? Because I *finally* had an idea of how much God loved me. I finally got it, in the true sense of God's love.

> He took my sins and my sorrows,
> He made them His very own;
> He bore my burden to Calv'ry,
> And suffered and died alone.
>
> How marvelous, how wonderful
> And my song shall ever be.
> How marvelous, how wonderful
> Is my Savior's love for me.

On the cross Jesus took not only our sins but our sorrows and our hurts and made them His own! Why? Because He is a masochist? No! Because He loved us, even before we ever were and before we ever loved Him. Even before our hurts, suffering, and pain ever came to be. Knowing that we would turn away, knowing that we would hurt Him, knowing that some of us would never come to know Him at all. He still took all of them. And not only that, but He did it all *alone*! He was separated from God, abandoned by His friends. In order to offer us forgiveness and salvation, Jesus took our eternal punishment. The ultimate get-out-of-jail-free card. He took our heavy baggage onto Himself and *suffered and died alone*. It absolutely broke my heart. So how can we not sing, "Jesus loves me, this I know"? How marvelous, how wonderful!

Author Darlene Sala writes, "I can judge my situation by what I know to be true about God, instead of judging God by my situation." Read that again, because this is something that is so important: *judge your situation by what you know to be true about God, instead of judging God by your situation*. We are able to find refuge in His love for us because, while everything else around us may fail, His love for us never will, and nothing can separate us from that love. Paul conveys that promise to us in Romans 8:35-37. "Can anything ever separate us from Christ's love? Does it mean He no longer loves us if we have trouble or calamity, or are persecuted, or hungry, or destitute, or in danger, or threatened with death? . . . No, despite all these things, overwhelming victory is ours through Christ, who loved us." When we finally understand this, it changes everything.

So be honest, do you believe that? Do you believe that God loves you? Acknowledge that you have ignored His love. Tell Him that you are trusting in what Christ did on your behalf. Won't you accept His love and His forgiveness of your sins? Won't you rely on Him instead of on yourself? I would encourage you to take a moment right now if you can't bring yourself to accept this gift of love and reread Ephesians 3:16-19. Then close your eyes and ask the Lord to speak His love into your heart.

I pray that from His glorious, unlimited resources He will empower you with inner strength through His Spirit. Then Christ will make His home in your hearts as you trust Him. Your roots will grow down into God's love and keep you strong. And may you have the power to understand, as all God's people should, how wide, how long, how high, and how deep His love is. May you experience the love of Christ, though it is too great to understand fully. (Eph. 3:16-19 NLT)

You Are Not Alone

❦

God whispers to us in our pleasures, speaks in our conscience, but shouts in our pain.

—C. S. Lewis

For God has said, "I will never fail you. I will never abandon you."

—Hebrews 13:5 NLT

A doctor speaks. A prognosis is given. An "I am sorry" is offered. The blood coursing through your veins feels as if it turns to ice. Suddenly everything around you fades to black. Your chest constricts, and you are gasping for air to fill lungs that refuse to be filled. *Grief* doesn't touch what you are feeling. *Fear* is a much smaller word than what you are experiencing. Have you been there? Maybe yours came in the form of a phone call, a knock on the door, or maybe it found you in complete and absolute silence. It doesn't really matter how it came but it did, and now you find yourself in survival mode. You find yourself thinking, *this is it. I am done. No more, please, God, no more.* This is the valley . . . deep. The valley . . . dark. The valley . . . dreadful.

First, *grief.* Defined as a multifaceted response to loss, particularly to the loss of someone or something to which a bond was formed. A clinical term that is cold and used to describe a "process." This is not the grief I am talking about. The type of grief that I am talking about is anything but clinical or process-driven. I am talking about an extreme mixture of the past and the future colliding in our present. Our hearts break for what was and what never will be. Not for the faint of heart, this is the soul-wrenching, tear-your-clothes-before-God, keep-your-tears-in-a-vial kind of grief. This is Holy Saturday grief, when God seems silent.

Holy Saturday, Jesus lies dead in a tomb, crucified. The disciples must have been heartsick. They had left everything behind to follow Jesus. They thought they were going to rule in a new kingdom with Him. Now He was dead, and they were left hiding and wondering, *what next?* I am sure they recalled memory after memory of miracles witnessed, Peter walking on the water, feeding the thousands with just a few fish and loaves of bread, the look on Mary's and Martha's faces as Lazarus emerged from the tomb. The times they shared a meal together, and all of the lessons He taught them as they shared life. And now as the hours passed after His death, they must have been thinking, *for what? Why?* And then, on Sunday evening as the disciples were gathered together, hiding behind locked doors, fearing what the Jewish leaders would do to them, Jesus appeared among them. The disciples' jaws must have dropped in disbelief. How quickly they had forgotten the promises that Jesus had made before His death. As soon as life got a little hairy, the promises Jesus made were forgotten, and the disciples must have begun to formulate plan B, a plan that depended solely on their abilities and completely left God out of the equation, a plan for self-preservation. But then Jesus appeared, and He offered them what every suffering person needs, peace. Suddenly Jesus was standing there among them! "'Peace be with you,' He said" (John

20:19 NLT). It changed everything for the disciples, and it changes everything for us as well. Have you found yourself there? Hiding from life as the disciples were and thinking, *for what, what next* and the biggest one of all, *why?* God seems to be silent, and the only things that seem present are desperation, fear, and nothingness. If that is where you are today, raise your eyes and see that Jesus is standing among you and is offering you peace.

> *"I am leaving you with a gift—peace of mind and heart.*
> *And the peace I give is a gift the world cannot give. So don't*
> *be troubled or afraid" (John 14:28 NLT).*

> *"Now may the Lord of peace himself give you His peace at*
> *all times and in every situation" (2 Thess. 3:16 NLT).*

> *"For Christ himself has brought peace to us"*
> *(Eph. 2:14a, NLT).*

God's peace, a peace that calms a tormented, grief-ridden soul. A peace that is available only through the soothing voice of Jesus. The promise that we can rest in is this: God's peace and the comfort it offers can and will sustain us in our times of suffering and trials. In the Sermon on the Mount, Jesus said, "Blessed are those who mourn, for they will be comforted" (Matt. 5:4 NIV). God gives hope to all of those who suffer from a broken heart by assuring both His abiding presence and His overflowing peace. Psalm 34:18 says, "The Lord is close to the brokenhearted and saves those who are crushed in spirit." God blesses us with a love that is greater than we can comprehend. In times of suffering, He beckons us to throw ourselves into His arms and let His presence comfort our wounded heart.

I have learned to cling to this peace, to abide in God's promise of comfort. To the world, this peace is difficult to understand, but without it and my faith in the God who provides it, doubt, worry, fear, anger, and red-hot searing pain would have overtaken my thoughts and eaten me alive. There would have been no hope, no purpose. Not behind losing our unborn son or facing such an unknown, incurable disease.

Next, *fear* . . . a basic survival mechanism, fight or flight, the things that nightmares are made of. You try to wake yourself up to make it all go away. You want to run but are frozen in place by terror at the oncoming light of what you know is a train barreling straight down the tracks at you. You are helpless to escape. You are one of the disciples huddled in the boat as the waves of the raging storm beat and batter them. The blackness of night envelops you, making it impossible to see where you are heading. You are soaked to the bone, weary to your core. The waves are smashing over the sides of the boat, making it impossible to make any progress forward. The wind is howling ferociously, making anything less than a shout unheard. You have probably never felt so alone—when suddenly you look out into the crashing waves and unbelievably see someone walking toward you. It is Jesus, who tells you, "Don't be afraid, take courage. I am here!"

Found 365 times in the Bible, "don't be afraid" is the most oft-repeated phrase. God's message for us—do not be afraid, have no fear—is the voice we most need to hear when we aren't able to move forward, paralyzed by our fear, when it is so dark around us we aren't able to see where we are heading, when no one seems to hear our cries for help above the howling winds. And why should we have no fear? Because of the second part of what Jesus says. God hears our cries, and He is with us. Just as Jesus was there to calm the seas for the disciples, God will calm our hearts amid the storm in our lives. God is there in the inky darkness of the valley. "Do not be afraid. I am here."

> *"So do not fear, for I am with you; do not be dismayed, for I am your God. I will strengthen you and help you. I will uphold you with my righteous right hand"* (Isa. 41:10).

This verse offers an abundance of comfort, peace, and encouragement to anyone who is fearful, weak, or distraught. When life happens and we are scared to death, this verse promises the love of a God that is all-sufficient, even in the worst of times. "Fear not, for I am with you," not just within shouting distance, not a phone call away, but with you, right beside you, within you, carrying you. "Do not be dismayed for I am God." He is bigger than anything we will ever have to face. Are you weak? He will strengthen you. He will help you in your time of need. Have you fallen? He promises to hold you up in His hand. God promises to take us by our hands as our guide, and to lead us, to be our strength when we are weak, to hold us up. When we are wavering, He will encourage us; when we are trembling, He will steady us. He will silence our fears. He promises it again and again through Scripture.

Exodus 14:13-14 says, "Don't be afraid. Just stand still and watch the Lord rescue you today. The Lord himself will fight for you." Moses is telling the Israelites as they faced the Red Sea on one side and the advancing Egyptian army on the other side, "Do not be afraid, stand firm, don't give up, just get out of the way and watch God work." I love that! As I faced a future with Takayasu's arteritus, I was afraid, and I prayed over and over that God would rescue me and He did. Maybe not in the way that I thought He would or should, but He has given me more strength, more sanity, more of Him, than I ever had before I was sick; I wouldn't trade any of that for the busy that I had before. It doesn't matter what you are facing, not only can we count on God to fight for us, we can also count on Him to rescue us.

Isaiah 43:2 says, "*When* you pass through the waters, I will be with you; and *when* you pass through the rivers, they will not sweep over you. *When* you walk through the fire, you will not be burned; the flames will not set you ablaze" (NIV, emphasis mine). Notice in this verse it says *when* you face trouble, not *if*. We are going to have bad days, weeks, years even. The question is: when you find yourself there, where do you turn?

We all face trials, hurts, suffering, and Jesus understands our journey through these deep waters. During His days here on earth, Jesus himself was tired, lonely, hurt, hated, beaten, rejected, persecuted, misunderstood and mistreated, mocked and laughed at, betrayed, tempted, and condemned. He has felt forsaken, lost loved ones, and experienced pain. He understands how it feels to be separated from God.

*Therefore, it was necessary for Him (Jesus) to be made
in every respect like us, His brothers and sisters, so that
He could be our merciful and faithful High Priest before
God. Then He could offer a sacrifice that would take away
the sins of the people. Since He himself has gone through
suffering and testing, He is able to help us when we are
being tested. (Heb. 2:17-18 NLT)*

Imagine Jesus in the garden of Gethsemane. It is late at night,
Jesus Himself is walking through the shadowy valley, and He has
the disciples with Him. He knows the time is coming for His death
and the fate that awaits Him. Jesus says His "soul is crushed with
grief to the point of death" (Matt. 26:38 NLT). He is distraught,
anguished, tormented.

*"My Father! If it is possible, let this cup of suffering be taken
away from me. Yet I want your will to be done, not mine"
(Matt. 26:39 NLT).*

This cup Jesus is begging to have removed contains in it all the
sins of humanity, your sin and mine. He was the perfect lamb being
brought to slaughter as the perfect sacrifice. Naturally, Jesus shrank
from what lay before Him, though He willingly submitted to it. He
cared so much for us that before we ever were, He sacrificed His life
in place of ours. He accepted the punishment for our crimes. Jesus,
in one moment in time, took on all of the suffering of the world.

As He returned from praying, He found His disciples asleep,
not one time but three times. Can you imagine? As Jesus is on His

face in prayer, in His agony, sorrowful and heavy, they couldn't even stay awake. "Couldn't you watch with me even one hour?" (Matt. 26:40 NLT) Jesus asks Peter as He returns the first time. His best friends, the ones He was looking to for comfort, deserted Him in His hour of need.

Does your soul feel as if it is crushed to the point of death? Has someone you counted on let you down? Let Jesus take your cup from you. He has been where you stand today and can relate to what you are going through. Look again at Isaiah 43:2 and the promise that God makes to you: "I will be with you." He wants to give you hope and walk with you through whatever pain you are experiencing. If we suffer with Christ, we shall reign with Him; and if we hope to reign with Him, why should we not expect to suffer with Him?

> So be truly glad. There is wonderful joy ahead, even though you have had to endure many trials for a little while. These trials will show that your **faith is genuine**. It is being tested as fire tests and purifies gold—though your faith is far more precious than mere gold. So when your faith remains strong through many trials, **it will bring you much praise and glory and honor** on the day when Jesus Christ is revealed to the whole world. (1 Peter 1:6-7 NLT, emphasis mine)

Strength enshrined in weakness, power in pain. This defies and undermines the human approach. It's hard sometimes even for me to wrap my mind around that fact, but I have found that Christ's peace is not a denial of my circumstances but instead, a commitment to the fact that God is enough for my situation and circumstances. This is genuineness of faith, the very definition of what true faith is.

Are you hiding, desperately trying to figure out a plan B? Are you screaming and feel like no one is listening—no one hears? Remember you are not alone; raise your eyes. Jesus is among us. God is listening and hears you.

Your Pain Has a Purpose

‿∾

If there is anything a sufferer needs, it is not an explanation, but a fresh, new look at God.

—Don Barker, Pain's Hidden Pleasure

When we find ourselves beat up and down, our wounds from our "valley walking" still fresh, the last thing we want is someone standing above us with his or her finger wagging, preaching to us with an "I told you so" or "I hope you learned your lesson." When we are hurting, we want someone to sit down next to us, take our hand, and tell us it's going to be okay, even if he or she doesn't really believe it. We want to pretend, at least for a little while, that everything is all right. That in that very moment in time, everything is fine, and all that has happened or is yet to happen will just go away—the hurt, the shame, the fear, the consequences. In the absence of being able to turn the clock back, in the absence of being able to change the course our life has taken, we want comfort. We want to be loved and assured. And many times, the last thing we want to hear is that our pain has a purpose. We want to wallow in our pain; we want to have a pity party for ourselves. We want to scream at God that He has made a mistake and demand that He fix it. God doesn't make mistakes, and search as we may for an escape route, the nearest exit as it were, from our current situation, it is in these situations that we really begin to understand what God is really like. I have been there, desperately searching for the emergency exit, but though we may not want to accept it, what we are going through has a purpose—God's Word tells us exactly that. If you are there today, I pray as I write this that God's words will penetrate your heart and you will be able to see God through the haze of your pain.

> *"And we know that God causes everything to work together*
> *for the good of those who love God and are called according*
> *to His purpose for them" (Rom. 8:28 NLT).*

Has anyone ever quoted you this Bible verse as if to say, "Don't worry. Everything will be fine. God will take this situation and make it all better. He will fix whatever (insert sickness, grief, problem here)." This Bible verse is very often quoted by Christians as a Band-Aid, as a promise that everything will work out for good. While that is exactly what this verse does promise, we have to look at the word *good* in the context of what God considers good to understand exactly what He is promising. If we back up and read the verses immediately preceding verse 28, it will help us see a clearer picture of "good."

> *And the Holy Spirit helps us in our weakness. For example,*
> *we don't know what God wants us to pray for. But the Holy*
> *Spirit prays for us with groanings that cannot be expressed*

in words. And the Father who knows all hearts knows what
the Spirit is saying, for the Spirit pleads for us believers in
harmony with God's own will. *And we know that God*
causes everything to work together for the good of those who
love God and are called according to His purpose for them.
(Rom. 8:26-28 NLT, emphasis mine)

In other words, God's purpose is to create Christlike character in us, to bring us into harmony with His will for us. He is interested in a "better us," not in providing an easier path. Sometimes we need the valleys to bring us nearer to God and remove our worldly attitudes. Verse 28 says that God causes *everything* to work together for our good. I understand this in these terms. A doctor works to heal someone using various methods, medications, tests, and procedures, not always pleasant but working together toward healing and health. The side effects of my medications that were reining my disease in and making me well in actuality made me feel worse in the immediate days following my diagnosis than I had when I was "sick." These side effects are part of the healing process, a consequence of that which is making us well. God wants to make us "well" through His power and grace. If we can cope with the side effects of our "medication," He will work in us, with us, and through us, and in the end the glory that will be revealed will be beautiful.

Believers, those who love God and are called by Him, those who trust in God, endure suffering with the confidence that this suffering comes under the control of an all-powerful and all-loving God. Our suffering has a meaning and a purpose in God's eternal plan, and He brings, or allows, this suffering into our lives only if it is for His glory and our good. For Jesus, the path to glory was the path of suffering. It isn't any different for us.

I have come to know God as I never had before, and I have come to realize that I had gotten really good at "talking the talk" but had no idea what the walk was all about. I had plans for my family and myself and felt that I was going about my life with God's blessing. I thought *He* was onboard with *my* plans. Remember that center guide bar I told you about? Here it was again with a jolt to get back on the right path. It is not enough to know God. Knowing God is the easy part. We have to trust God unfalteringly.

Have you ever felt like Job? Poor Job got blindsided by Satan as one tragedy after another struck him. After having lived a life where he served God devoutly and was in turn greatly blessed by the Lord, Satan entered Job's life to test him, with the Lord's permission, and took from him everything in an attempt to destroy him and make him denounce the name of the Lord. Blow after blow, he lost everything: his children were killed, his possessions and his wealth were taken, and finally even his health came under attack. He was completely broken down, but Job in the midst of all of his misery, asked this question: "Should we accept only good things from the hand of God and never anything bad?" (Job 2:10 NLT). What an amazing servant, faith-minded attitude. I desire to have an attitude more like Job's, to be an example of suffering affliction and of patience. Throughout everything that Satan threw at Job, Job remained steadfast in his faith, blessing God, asking the above question and proving himself an honest man.

God has a greater purpose than our immediate comfort. Getting what we want, when we want it, is not always best for us, or glorifying to God. Just as Mary and Martha had to be brought to a point of complete and absolute helplessness and hopelessness before Jesus raised their brother, Lazarus, from the dead, we too must face helplessness and hopelessness so that we may focus on God, putting all of our faith in Him alone, giving Him an opportunity to demonstrate in an unmistakable way that His power and grace are sufficient for all of our needs. We need to learn to let go and let God. We think God needs our help, and the truth is He doesn't. We get caught up in the worry and fear and anxiety that life throws at us like they are our job. All three of those things place us in direct opposition to where we are supposed to be in our walk with God because they are all seated in doubt—doubt in God and His power to rescue us. Doubt in God's promise to pick us up and tend to our valley injuries. Genuine worship and thanksgiving through the suffering and trials in our lives come from actually knowing and trusting in the goodness of God. God's plans for us are bigger than our plans are for us. We must trust Him when we can't see the big picture or the end of the story, because there *is* glory ahead.

"I consider that our present sufferings are not worth comparing with the glory that will be revealed in us" (Rom. 8:18 NIV).

These are great words of encouragement from Paul, a man who understood all too well what suffering was, not just for suffering's sake but suffering for Christ. In our painful present, we may feel anything but glorious as we continue down our darkened path. God, however, trades the sufferings we experience today for a great and eternal glory, one that can't compare to our "present sufferings." So Paul's encouragement is to continue on, there are greater things to come. Second Corinthians 4:17 says this: "For our light and momentary troubles are achieving for us an eternal glory that far outweighs them all" (NIV). It is a matter of comparison. A car is heavy, especially when it comes to rest on your foot. But it is light in comparison to the planet. This is momentary trouble compared with eternal glory. I know that there are days when our troubles feel anything but light and momentary; they feel crushing and endless. We don't see any way out. Those are the days when we need to immerse ourselves in God's Word, in God's promises of what is to come.

I have come to realize that sometimes bad things are going to happen. Sometimes terrible, unthinkable, unimaginable things are going to happen, but *it is* God's will. He has not turned His back on me, and I can use these things to make me bitter or I can use them to make me better. I love what Charles Spurgeon says; maybe you too can identify with his words. "I bear my willing witness that I owe more to the fire, and the hammer, and the file, than to anything else in my Lord's workshop. I sometimes question whether I have ever learned anything except through the rod. When my schoolroom is darkened, I see most."

You may still be asking, how can God take what I am going through and make it good? There is no way that this can end well. You don't understand the depth of my loss, the magnitude of my hurt. I would tell you that when you find yourself at that threshold of helplessness and hopelessness, if you choose to turn to God as your source of comfort and strength, your source of help and hope, *you have found the good.* If in your losses you can learn to trust God for everything, *you have found the good.* The situation may not end immediately, but in the very act of turning to God, *you have found the good.* In leaning on God and allowing His grace to carry you through, *you have found the good.* This is a choice we must make; it is an all-in attitude. We can't live in the gray area if we hope to find the good in the midst of suffering. We can't split our loyalties; God wants all of us.

In his book *Forgotten God,* Francis Chan says, "When we are referring to God, balance is a huge mistake. God is not just one thing we add to the mix called life. He wants an invitation from us to permeate everything and every part of us." If you continue to look to the world for answers, the "good" will continue to elude you. We have to again look at Romans 8:28 and remember what God considers "good" and also remember it is God who causes this. This is not about us or anything we can do within our own power. This is about God. He is the one who takes the bad and makes it good, takes the ugly and makes it beautiful, takes the valleys of my life and creates a story that glorifies Him.

Strength Will Rise as We Wait upon the Lord

Trust God when He puts you in the waiting room. He knows what He's doing.

—Charles Stanley

Let all that I am wait quietly before God, for my hope is in Him. He alone is my rock and my salvation, my fortress where I will not be shaken.

—Psalm 62:5-6 NLT

Have you ever felt like you were on hold with God? Have you prayed so desperately for something and felt like God just wasn't listening? One night not long after my diagnosis as I was praying for healing and answers, I chuckled to myself as I thought about being on hold with God. I could hear the bad jazz music in my head, and a soothing canned voice repeating, "We are experiencing an unusually high prayer volume tonight, but your prayer is very important to God. Please continue to hold, and your prayer will be answered in the order it was received." Thankfully that isn't the way it works, but sometimes it feels as if we have been put on hold.

Since my diagnosis, I have been doing a lot of waiting—waiting on test results, waiting on medical answers, and waiting on God. I don't like to wait—I don't know many people who do—not at the grocery store, not in traffic, and not at the doctor's office. We are programmed to want what we want, when we want it, and to go, go, go. We want answers now. A peak behind the curtain, so to speak, to see what God has in store. We would like to be able to move on to the next chapter in our lives, continue down the path, but instead we often find ourselves waiting.

When troubles come, crisis mode will invariably pass and leave behind the wait. I am good in crisis mode: faith kicks in and a plan is made. Crisis mode equals action. I am not so good in patience mode. How well do you do when you are told to wait for something? Especially when what you are waiting for involves such a desperate, strong request made of God? I understand with my head that God has a plan and the timing for everything must be His, but that doesn't mean that it isn't difficult for my heart. My head knows that we learn some of life's greatest lessons through delayed gratification. Good things are worth waiting for, right? God is all-powerful, He knows our every desire, need, wish, and prayer. He already has everything planned and prepared for us. It takes courage to do nothing, especially for white-knuckle, control freaks like me. Waiting implies that we aren't in control, and it becomes very desirable to try to manipulate things by our own power. But what can we do apart from God? We will miss out on what God wants to do for us if we try to do it on our own. And He has big plans for us, through His power, in His time. While we are waiting, He is working.

My favorite Bible verse about waiting is Isaiah 40:31: "Those who wait on the Lord shall renew their strength; they shall mount up with wings like eagles, they shall run and not be weary, they shall walk and not faint" (NKJV). Isn't that a glorious picture? Mounting up with wings like eagles, strongly, swiftly, flying so high and heavenward. How many times have you felt so beaten down that you didn't have the strength to face another day? When we are in the valley . . . deep, the valley . . . dark, the valley . . . dreadful, it is hard to see anything else. We understand tired and weary to our very core. Walking and running, let alone soaring with the eagles, feels impossible. But this verse says that if we wait on the Lord, for Him to work His plan, all of those things will be restored to us. The Lord will become the source of our strength, of our endurance. The Lord will show you the path out of the valley. That power is worth the wait!

> *"Trust in the Lord with all your heart; do not depend on your own understanding. Seek His will in all you do, and He will show you which path to take"* (Prov. 3:5-6 NLT).

After losing our son, life returned to normal, albeit slowly. I had a family to raise and started a new business, and life rolled on, without an utter dependence on God. God was part of my life on a daily basis, but I was not dependent on God. I did my part while God did His part and the job got done, but I was missing out on the opportunity of a deep relationship with God, a true connection with Him.

One afternoon about a month after my diagnosis, I said to my nine-year-old daughter as we were driving down the road, "Isn't it amazing what God has been doing lately? He seems to be everywhere around us these days." I wasn't ready for her response. She looked at me and with seriousness said, "Mom, I think He has always been there; you just haven't seen Him." Out of the mouths of babes. Remember when I said I was busy? Satan had me right where he wanted me, out of the way. I was living life my way again, foolishly thinking my craziness was all in the name of God. I was so busy "doing" that I didn't have time to listen. And more importantly, follow.

To drive this point home even further, I found a letter entitled "This Thing Is from Me" while reading *A Bend in the Road* by David Jeremiah. It was like getting hit smack between the eyes. The letter is written from God's standpoint to someone who is in the midst of some kind of heartache. I want to share a portion of it . . .

> My child, I have a message for you today; let Me whisper it in your ear, that it may gild with glory any storm clouds which may arise, and smooth the rough places upon which you may have to tread. It is short—only five words—but let them sink into your inmost soul; use them as a pillow upon which to rest your weary head:
>
> THIS THING IS FROM ME.
>
> Have you longed to do some great work for Me, and instead been laid aside on a bed of pain and weakness? This thing is from Me. I could not get your attention in your busy days, and I want to teach you some of My deepest lessons.

I read that over and over and over. Could it be that God was trying to get my attention, and I wasn't listening? It was more than possible. It was probable. Sometimes in order to get our attention, God has to interrupt us, as good and godly as our plans may seem. He has to remove us from the distractions of what we think are an ideal life in order to show us something greater. Life's interruptions are God's way of getting us back on track.

Control is a very hard thing to give up, and God's lesson to me over and over has been that the control belongs to Him. (Sometimes I think maybe I am a slow learner.) I had created a nice life for myself and liked it just the way it was. It had been very easy to say, "Yes, God is in control of my life . . . now here is what He wants me to do." That, however, was not God's plan.

Once I released this control to God completely, there was a weight that was immediately lifted from my shoulders. I realized that worrying over what might be is a strength-draining activity, because not only is it pointless, but it is oftentimes depressing. Psalm 55:22 instructs us to "give your burdens to the Lord, and He will take care of you" (NLT). This release of control is something that I continue to struggle with, and every day, sometimes multiple times a day, I have to make an effort to give God control. We are missing out on what God wants to do for us when we try to do it on our own. It is not just enough to know God. Knowing God is the easy part. We have to trust God unfalteringly. When I got to this point in my walk, I became free—free from worry, free from anxiety, free to live my life in the knowledge that I am not alone, no matter where my path may lead. I challenge you right now to stop and take stock of the burdens you are attempting to carry on your own. Release them to God, give Him your burdens, and allow Him to take care of you.

> *"He tends His flock like a shepherd: He gathers the lambs*
> *in His arms and carries them close to His heart; He gently*
> *leads those that have young" (Isa. 40:11 NIV).*

It is said that when a shepherd is trying to lead his flock up an especially treacherous path and they won't follow, the shepherd will reach into the flock, taking a lamb in each arm, and start up the path. Eventually the two mother sheep will follow the shepherd, and then behind them will come the rest of the flock. This story then goes on to say that sometimes God will take a lamb in order to lead us to Him.

Did God take our little lamb because we weren't following Him? What a devastating thought. God couldn't use me before this heartbreak, when I was trying to do it on my own. It wasn't until I was broken and searching for Him out of the depths of the valley that He was able to use me to glorify Him. Has God chosen this rare, incurable disease to ensure my life never goes back to the "state of busy"? To ensure my eyes are always focused on Him? As you hit bottom, there is only one direction to look . . . up. God doesn't just want us when times are good. He wants us all the time. We need to learn to live every day, good and bad, desperate for God.

There are times in our lives when we need to "lean not on our own understanding" and trust in God to bring to fruition what is in our best interest. Scripture is filled with references to the "due season" and "appointed time" of God's fulfillment. God is never too late . . . never too early, but always right on time. Sometimes, though, our clocks are not in sync. God was not asleep at the wheel the day we lost our son. My diagnosis of Takayasu's arteritus did not take Him by surprise. Dr. Dobson, in *When God Doesn't Make Sense*, wrote, "Clearly unless the Lord chooses to explain Himself to us, which often He does not, . . . Many of our questions, especially those that begin with the word why, will have to remain unanswered for the time being."

I often wonder what my son would have been like. I wonder what his personality would have been like as he grew and matured, and whom he would have looked like. With God's help, though, I have escaped the what-if trap that Satan would love to ensnare me in. What if we had known that there was the possibility that we would lose our son? Would I have done anything differently? Would there have been a chance to save him? And if he were born at thirty-two weeks, what maladies would he have suffered? Would he have lived a second? A minute? A day, week, or year? And how much harder would that have been to see him suffering and in pain? Isn't it better that God took him when He did? These what-ifs are rooted in doubt and self-destruction. Not just in self-doubt, but in doubt of God and in His power and grace and timing.

Timing, waiting, and the endurance to see it through are all necessary elements to consider in the development of any vision. Think of a jigsaw puzzle, one in which you are only able to see a few of the pieces at a time, one in which you have no idea what the final product is going to look like. How could you ever put it together? You wouldn't even know where to begin. So it is with our lives. We don't always understand God's timing. God knows what the final picture is going to be, though. He knows best which pieces go where, so it makes sense that we should allow Him to piece together our lives and trust that the end result is going to be a beautiful picture.

God speaks to us in such amazing ways. One early morning in April, three months after being diagnosed with Takayasu's arteritus, He scored a direct hit. I was on my way to the Cleveland Clinic for an MRI—the first MRI since my body had been sabotaged with massive doses of steroids, the MRI that we had been fervently praying would show a miracle, the MRI that I hoped would show that all signs of the inflammation were not only gone, but there was not even evidence that they ever existed. I had opened my Bible app on my phone to reread the story in Matthew 9:20-22, where an ill woman reaches out and touches Jesus' robe in the belief that she will be healed, and because of her faith and Jesus' amazing love, she was, a story that had brought me much hope and comfort in the days leading up to this test. But before I could even get there, I read the verse of the day . . .

> *"And the God of all grace, who called you to His eternal*
> *glory in Christ, after you have suffered a little while,*
> *will himself restore you and make you strong, firm, and*
> *steadfast" (1 Peter 5:10 NIV).*

There are no words to describe how amazing it is when God speaks to you, through the Word, through the Holy Spirit, or through others. It is awe-inspiring and overwhelming and comforting. I read that verse, and to the very core of my soul knew that God was promising *me* that it would be okay and I would be okay. No matter what that test said, or the next test, or the one after that, I had a promise: that I would be restored. The New Living Translation version says, "He will support, and strengthen you, and place you on a firm foundation," and He already has.

I didn't get my miracle on that day, but I did get an answer to my prayer: there was no active disease. I know that God has a plan, and while the future is as unknown to me today as it was yesterday, God is already there, He already knows what will happen, and He is waiting for me. I am not going to quit hoping for a miracle, that there will be no evidence of this disease, but if that never happens, I won't ever lose faith in the fact that God has me in the palm of His hand and will continue to protect me while He continues to use me. God wants us to give Him our hopes and dreams and to trust Him to work the miracles necessary to bring them about without our interference.

David Bloom, NBC news commentator, husband, father of three, and Christian, chose to go to Iraq during Operation Iraqi Freedom and was embedded with a military unit. One morning, climbing out of the armored vehicle that he had been traveling in, he collapsed. He was rushed to a medical unit but was dead on arrival from a pulmonary embolism. His last e-mail to his wife was published in *People* magazine and read as follows:

> You can't begin to fathom, cannot begin to even glimpse the enormity of the changes I have and am continuing to undergo. God takes you to the depths of your being, until you're at rock bottom, and then, if you turn to Him with utter blind faith and resolve in your heart and mind to walk only with Him and

towards Him, picks you up with your bootstraps and leads you home.

At the memorial service in Manhattan, David's wife read e-mail after e-mail depicting her husband's deep faith. Among those assembled were leaders from the media, government, entertainment moguls, prominent citizens, family, and friends— many of whom didn't know of David's faith until then. David brought a message of salvation and faith to many across the globe through his death, ministering to millions more than he could have alive. Again, God's timing is not always ours, and sometimes He has bigger plans for us, but we may have to make the ultimate sacrifice.

Through His grace, God will never ask you to do something you can't do without His help. To say yes to God may mean saying no to what we want. To say yes to embracing my disease and proclaiming God's glory, though it goes against the grain of society. This is not God's will my way, but God's will God's way. We are called to action, called to follow Christ, to live within His will, and that doesn't always line up with our plans for ourselves. We are all gifted and skilled, and God wants to use those things, with and through His power for His glory. We just have to make ourselves available to Him.

If you find yourself feeling like you are stuck on hold, realize God is working, and take the time that He is giving you to rest, to prepare, so that when the wait is over, you are able to run and not get tired, to walk and not become weary.

Finding the Grace for Endurance

✑

So let us come boldly to the throne of our gracious God. There we will receive His mercy, and we will find grace to help us when we need it most.

—*Hebrews 4:16 NLT*

We can rejoice, too, when we run into problems and trials, for we know that they help us develop endurance. And endurance develops strength of character, and character strengthens our confident hope of salvation. And this hope will not lead to disappointment. For we know how dearly God loves us, because He has given us the Holy Spirit to fill our hearts with His love.

—*Romans 5:3-5 NLT*

Endurance, also called sufferance, is defined as the ability or strength to continue or last, especially despite fatigue, stress, or other adverse conditions. It is the ability to resist, withstand, recover from, and have immunity to wounds.

Endurance . . . the long haul. Life is not a sprint, but a marathon. For endurance runners, those crazy athletes who compete in races such as the Marathon Des Sables, in the Sahara Desert, where they run 151 miles or 243K, it truly is a long haul. How do people even get to a place where they are able to compete in such an elite and physically demanding contest? Their preparation through training, both physical and mental, getting the proper nourishment before, during, and then after the race, staying hydrated, and even having the right equipment are vital. In addition to all of those things, experience also plays a major role. It takes time to become a world-class endurance runner, and there are no shortcuts.

Have you ever felt like you were thrown into the middle of one of those races? I know that I did, and I found myself unable to muster the energy from within to continue for very long on my own. I felt like I was in the middle of the Sahara Desert, tired, my feet blistered and aching, gasping for air as my heart raced, and all I wanted to do was to stop running. But that was when my training kicked in. Our training comes in the form of a relationship with God, digging into His Word for nourishment, and spending time in prayer, communication with our Father, allowing Him to pour down endurance for us, physically and mentally, in order to continue on. Endurance doesn't come without training.

Without endurance, it is easy to throw in the towel when we get tired, scared, or hurt. What if Paul had given up? Can you imagine him saying, "Thanks for your confidence in me, God. I know that you have this great plan, but really, I am tired of being beaten, stoned, and imprisoned. There has got to be more to this life than this abuse. I believe in your cause and all, but let someone else spread the word. This life is not for me." The external circumstances that we find ourselves unable to control are God's way of building our endurance and our character; at the same time, He is working within us to provide the strength to not only survive whatever we are facing but to make us more effective for whatever plans He may have for us.

I have learned that we need to be in constant training because we never know when we are going to find ourselves in the middle of a marathon of crisis. This notion became very clear to me not long ago. I had just finished speaking to a group of about a hundred ladies at a Mother's Day brunch on how God can take our messes and make them beautiful. As I sat back down at my table, I looked around the room, and a revelation hit me! As I was speaking, there was a group of ladies who were listening raptly, nodding, leaning in and waiting for the next nugget of truth that I was sharing. These ladies were in training. Then there was another group of ladies. These women were smiling politely, but they were there for entertainment purposes only—or perhaps for the nice breakfast. This was, after all, a women's ministry function so their presence must be made because otherwise, what might people think?

It was in this moment that I realized how many times I myself had sat in that seat. I would smile politely as well from the "observer's" seats (these are the seats that the crowd sits in while watching the athletes compete), while thinking smugly, "Thanks for your input. You have a very nice story, but I've got this." I may have even thought, "Wow, am I glad I am not you." I grew up in a solid Christian home, was involved in our church, prayed together with my family before meals and before bed, and my children were being brought up to love and fear the Lord. In other words, I may not have been in "ultra marathon runner shape," but I was more than a couch potato. Like I said before, I got it. Oh, foolish proud heart. Then God let me have it! And I realized that I had nothing without Him.

At that very moment, sitting in the audience as the brunch came to a close, I wanted to run back on stage and warn the women sitting there. I wanted to tell them to wake up before it was too late. They were treading a slippery slope, headed directly into oncoming traffic. I recognized it because I had been there. Their Christianity was in hibernation, only to be awakened in crisis. We need to use our "faith muscles" every day because if we wait until crisis strikes, they will be sluggish and sleepy when we need them most. We will have to dust our faith off and hope that we remember how to work it. Our hope will be that we will have the endurance to go from the laziness of the couch to the world-class svelteness of an ultra marathon runner. I have learned firsthand that God will use a crisis to get our attention.

Not long after receiving my diagnosis, I was searching for meaning in the chaos. My brain was trying to tie this disease up into a nice, neat little package and then be able to file it away; and in this process, I became still for the first time in a very long time. I began to quiet my mind—a mind that generally raced from one place to the next as quickly as my car did. When faced with a disease as unknown as Takayasu's arteritus and being forced to come to terms with your own mortality, your priorities shift and you realize what is real, what is important, what is worthy of your time and attention. God had my attention, He had my ear, He had my whole heart, and He was speaking. Not in the thunder, not in the earthquake, but in the quiet. That is where we will find God every time. And before long, He began moving. The week after I was diagnosed, God laid on my heart the need for a prayer team. I had a team of medical professionals tending to my physical worldly needs, but I wanted—and needed—a team of prayer warriors petitioning the throne of the Great Physician. Within hours, the prayer team had taken hold, and we had people praying across the country.

"From the depths of despair, O Lord, I call for your help. Hear my cry, O Lord. Pay attention to my prayer" (Ps. 130:1 NLT).

I have found the best way to live life is on your knees, especially when you find yourself in the middle of a storm. Prayer, however, is something that if we are honest, most of us struggle with. I did. Prayer, when we remember, is too often used as a last resort, or is a few hollow words uttered in passing, sometimes as we are driving down the road or hurriedly as we go about our daily routines. Our minds drift, and before long we are thinking about what we need from the store or what we are making for dinner. We find ourselves praying when all of our efforts have been exhausted, have come to nothing, and we have nowhere else to turn. If we are honest, we also find ourselves sometimes praying to avoid the consequences of the messes that we have created.

When we pray, when we are approaching the throne of God. We need to remember who we are praying to, who we are approaching, and this is why I say it's important to be on our knees. The God who created the heavens and the stars, parted the sea, tumbled the walls of Jericho, shut the lions' mouths, silenced the storm, made the blind to see, made the lame to walk, and emptied the tomb forever, is listening to my prayers, to your prayers, and *He cares*! I will say that again, because I know I need to hear it continually; I think we all do. *God cares for us, and He is listening!* And more than listening and answering, prayer is a way for God to talk to us. Through prayer, God is able to encourage us, to lift us up, to provide the grace to continue on. James 4:8 says, "Come close to God, and God will come close to you" (NLT). When was the last time that you found yourself more discouraged after spending time with God in prayer? It doesn't happen. First we pray, and then we listen for that still, small voice.

One night in late February, we were having this conversation with our kids at dinner. We were talking about the seriousness with which we need to approach prayer and the power that we have through it. That night as I got down on my knees beside my daughter's bed, as I do every night, I asked her what she wanted to pray for. She thought about it and said a two-hour delay for school. So she got down on her knees beside me, and we prayed. When I was putting my son to bed, I told him what we had prayed for, and he said he too had gotten on his knees and prayed for the same thing. That night as I went to bed, I said my own prayer. "Please, Lord, I know that you are able to grant my children's prayers, and we spent time talking tonight about the power that is available to us through prayer. It would be such an amazing lesson if you would grant them their requests." Now we all prayed these prayers knowing that there wasn't any significant snow in the forecast, which made what happened the next morning even more amazing.

At 5:18 a.m.—yes, I remember the time exactly—I woke up to the phone ringing. It was the school district's automated service, letting us know they were operating on a two-hour delay. But our kids go to school in another district, so I waited about ten minutes without hearing from their school and then checked the Internet. At 5:30 a.m., there were two schools that were operating on a two-hour delay, the district that we lived in and the district where my kids go to school. That was it! I wanted to scream it from the rooftops that God had taken such a small and seemingly unimportant request and used it to show two children, and their parents, what can happen when we get on our knees and pray. I couldn't wait for them to wake up so that I could tell them. This was the living proof of what Matthew 21:22 says: "You can pray for anything, and if you have faith, you will receive it" (NLT). That morning we all got on our knees again and thanked Him, and they decided they should have just asked for a snow day! Isn't our God awesome?

Galatians 6:9 says, "So let's not get tired of doing what is good. At just the right time we will reap a harvest of blessing if we do not give up" (NLT) Keep your eyes fixed on God instead of your struggles and be ready to run out into your future, knowing that God is already there and has prepared it for you. "The longer the blessing is in coming," Charles Spurgeon said, "the richer it will be when it arrives. That which is gained speedily by a single prayer is sometimes only a second-rate blessing; but that which is gained after many a desperate tug and many an awful struggle, is a full-weighted and precious blessing. That which costs us the most prayer will be worth the most."

There are some trials in life that we are just not going to be able to escape, no matter how hard we try or how far we run. When we pray, when we engage God, we are bringing Him into the middle of our battle. Do you want your battling to be in vain? As long as we stay on our knees, God will be battling right alongside of us, providing unlimited access to that power that He is longing to provide. Let God become your running companion, and I promise you will find yourself able to run farther and faster than you ever thought possible.

When You Are Weak,
Then You Are Strong

Each time He [the Lord] said, "My grace is all you need. My power works best in weakness." So now I am glad to boast about my weakness, so that the power of Christ can work through me. That's why I take pleasure in my weakness, and in the insults, hardships, persecution, and troubles that I suffer for Christ. For when I am weak, then I am strong.

—2 Corinthians 12:9-10 NLT

How foolish can you be? After starting your Christian lives in the Spirit, why are you now trying to become perfect by your own human effort? Have you experienced so much for nothing? Surely it was not in vain, was it?

—Galatians 3:3-4 NLT

I promised you complete honesty, and that is what I have delivered in every word and on every page—and now we reach this crossroad. I would love to tell you that I readily boast about my weakness, but I have days that I really struggle with vulnerability, more than I struggle with control, more than I struggle with trusting God with my tomorrows. And why? Pride. I never thought that I was a prideful person until God opened my eyes to see myself as He saw me.

The problem that I know I struggle with is becoming too easily complacent and self-sufficient. It becomes a slow fade from utter dependence on God every moment of every day, to "Oh yeah, hey, God, I could use you today. There is something I need (or probably more correctly, want)." Let me break down my walls of pride and tell you that God isn't interested in my eloquence as a speaker or a writer. He is only interested in my surrendered life. I am no good to Him—my message holds no weight—unless He, and He alone, is the author of it. And if I am brutally honest with myself as well as the rest of you, without a diagnosis of Takayasu's arteritus and the continuation of battling an incurable disease (which means no miracle of healing), my pride and self-sufficiency would still be running my life in secret. And my fear is that with a miracle, those worldly crutches would begin to eventually, over time, creep back into their supreme position.

Life hurts sometimes, no doubt about it. When it does, I have learned that I need to step past my pride and self-sufficiency and have the confidence in my weakness to ask for help when I need it and then have the humility to receive it on God's terms, so that His perfect strength can be displayed. We don't need to understand it; we don't need to agree with it. In fact, we don't have much choice in the matter if we are going to be obedient.

For a long time, I have felt that I needed to share the story that God is writing on my life with others. I felt that as long as I was able to do this, then my son's death wasn't for naught. The first time that I was given the opportunity to speak publicly (five years before I was diagnosed with Takayasu's arteritus), I was ecstatic. The closer the date came, though, the more I started becoming filled with a sense of dread and began putting off gathering my thoughts and speaking materials. My husband was going to Scottsdale, Arizona, for a long weekend on business, and I had planned to go with him, our first trip away together since we had had children. I decided that I would use this quiet time in the warm Arizona sun without interruption to pull together my thoughts. We were supposed to fly home on a Tuesday, and so on Monday (after too much time in the sun), when I finally couldn't put off the inevitable any longer, I said a prayer and jumped in with both feet. I made a startling revelation. Five years after my son's death, I had never fully dealt with it and had spent much of this time hiding behind my faith. For the first time in a long time, I had uninterrupted time with God. There were no phones to answer, meals to prepare, no toys to pick up, no children to tend to. It was just me, my Bible, and God sitting beneath a shade tree in Arizona.

Here is what I discovered. Eleven months after our son was stillborn, we had a daughter. In the three months between the death of our son and when I became pregnant again, I occupied myself with lavishing attention on our other son and starting a new career. Once we found out I was pregnant, I had another distraction, this time a major one. I was scheduled to be induced, and at thirty-six weeks, only four weeks further along than in my previous pregnancy, I entered the hospital once again. This time the outcome was much different; our daughter was born healthy and happy. I then had a new baby filling my arms, my thoughts, and my heart. I was hiding from the pain, and I filed the hurt away in a drawer deep inside and I didn't let it out. But there was that strong center bar again, jolting me back on track. The shadows from the valley had begun darkening the corners of my life as I had gotten comfortable.

On this Monday I had come face-to-face with myself and the pain that I hadn't let myself feel in a long time. The more I do, the less I feel; and the less I feel, the less I hurt. I thought I was doing just fine, that I had been handling myself in a healthy manner. I had been able to talk about my journey without having a complete breakdown, but I didn't realize that I had put up a major wall within myself, not allowing the emotion to spill over into the matter-of-fact way that I had dealt with this. I was afraid to be vulnerable, especially in the eyes of others, because in that I saw a weakness in myself. Repeatedly people had commented on my strength, but in reality, I tucked the pain and hurt away and never fully dealt with them. I hid behind God, keeping my emotions tightly in check.

We need to be living, compassionate human beings, not robots who in the face of tragedy simply say, "Well, that was not God's will for my life" and then get up, brush ourselves off, and move on with our lives. We need to feel, to grieve, and then to heal, and we need to allow God and others in to help us do that. God had taught me some powerful lessons about the importance of absolute faith in Him and Him alone during times of tragedy, but here I was years later, still the student, learning how to deal with the ripple effects of pride and self-sufficiency.

I was preparing to speak about my faith, and I was trying to do it on my own. My path had smoothed, the shadows were gone, I had gotten my feet back underneath me and was standing on solid ground—or so I thought. Instead, I found myself standing on a hidden fault line that opened into a huge fissure when God suddenly rocked my world.

Society today tells us that self-sufficiency is a desirable trait. Independence, self-reliance, autonomy—all desirable traits. I needed to learn that it is okay to be weak. It is okay to be vulnerable and not have all the answers, not to have it all together all the time, because when I don't, then God is able to provide all that I need and more. In Job, Bildad is speaking to Job about those who have forgotten God and the deadly trap that society sets when he says,

"What he trusts in is fragile; what he relies on is a spider's web. He leans on his web, but it gives way; he clings to it but it does not hold"(Job 8:14-15 NIV). God wants us to lean on Him, He does for us what we cannot do for ourselves. In our weakness, God has an opportunity to work in us and through us, giving us strength through His power, and the glory of our transformation belongs to Him alone.

As time had passed, I was turning this "strength" as I perceived it into a dangerous thing. In being strong, I cut myself off from my emotions, and in doing so created a safe place. I was able to absorb the emotions of those around me without having to actually have emotions of my own. Instead of fully allowing myself to feel the brunt of my pain, I had created a numbness and called it strength. I was afraid that if I felt the pain that I would also feel the anger, and I was afraid if I started down that road, I might not be able to come back. In my strength, I was robbing God of the ability to save me from myself and robbing myself of the knowledge and gift of true strength and dependence on God. God was longing to provide not the fake, plastered-smile, I-have-it-all-together façade that I was trying to convincingly pull off, but the glorious, holy power that brings with it pure strength.

Anger and bitterness are far more common than most of us would like to admit. Sometimes it just feels good to be angry, especially when we don't have the answers or they aren't the answers we wanted. It feels good to point fingers and place blame in order to try and make sense of things. We end up destroying our own soul when it becomes filled with anger, resentment, and hate; the one who has wronged us moves on, while we crumble under the weight of our resentment. It is hard to forgive sometimes, yet I have found it is even harder to carry the soul-crushing weight of anger and resentment.

Two months after our son died, just before Christmas, I became overcome with anger. I was soaking in a steaming hot tub one evening, and the longer I soaked, the madder I got. I began thinking that this wasn't fair. I was supposed to have two little boys this Christmas. We had planned to have sweet Christmas pictures of the boys taken as birth announcements. Instead, I had a broken heart. I threw on my robe and flew out of the bathroom, startling my husband, and with clenched fists began beating his chest telling him that, "This isn't fair!" I was so angry, and it felt good. He soothed me and listened to me, and that anger soon dissolved into tears.

Having feelings of anger is not a sin. In fact, Jesus demonstrated anger in His days here on earth, yet He did not sin. Of all of our emotions, anger is perhaps the rawest, strongest, and potentially most destructive. Unbridled anger must not be allowed to harbor in our hearts, where it can become the root of bitterness and resentment. Ephesians 4:26-27 says, "Don't sin by letting anger control you. Don't let the sun go down while you are still angry, for anger gives a foothold to the devil" (NLT). We must choose to be honest about our anger and admit that we feel that we've been let down, that life isn't fair, that we have been forgotten, passed over, and left for dead by those whom we loved the most. When we can take the first step in admitting these things, then we can begin to heal. Are you angry at God? Admitting that we are carrying this anger doesn't mean that He's guilty; God cannot commit sin. But when we admit and acknowledge our anger at God, we release our expectations of what we think God should have done to prevent our hurt or failure in the first place. When we acknowledge our anger at others and seek forgiveness for this anger, God creates in us a clean heart and renews our spirit, allowing us to begin living again.

Pierre Wolff in his book entitled *May I Hate God?* says, "Perhaps there is a hatred present as long as people are mute, but as soon as they decide to express what is in their hearts to the other, something is already changing and may have even already changed. This expression is a desire for reconciliation. If I can tell you, my friend, that I hate you, and if you can accept my words and feelings, then love is present, working and conquering. You are still alive and present in my life, even though in sorrow . . ." It is the not-speaking-our-hatred that deadens a relationship. When we withdraw in silence, relationships wither away. It is the same way in our relationship with God. If in our anger we withdraw from Him, our relationship with Him will suffer. God can handle your anger and will forgive you for your feelings. If you continue to stoke the flames of your anger, however, your heart will be hardened toward God and the rest of the world.

So it's time for a gut check. To do that, I need to refer back to Natalie Grant's song "Held," which I partially quoted at the very beginning of the book and the question that I asked. The second verse of the song says, "This hand is bitterness. We want to taste it and let the hatred numb our sorrows." The question is this: how are you? I know how I used to answer it. Are you holding on tightly to your bitterness, to your anger, letting your hatred numb the pain and sorrow and disappointment of what you think should have been? Have you driven a wedge between yourself and others who have reached out their hands to help because your pride wouldn't allow you to take it, wouldn't allow for vulnerability and weakness? Have you written God off because He didn't come to your rescue when you thought He should have? How often do we hold onto our disappointments and our anger? The injustices that we have suffered have become such a part of who we think we are that we can't let go of them. We don't want to let them go. They have become part of our identity, and we hold onto them because even though it may be painful, it is safe because we know what to expect, even if it is suffering and pain. We hold onto this mess because we feel like we deserve it, and life moving forward can be scary.

But my very first words to you were Natalie Grant's words: *This is what it is to be loved and to know that the promise was, when everything fell, we'd be held.*

Especially in your hurt and in your anger, God is reaching out to you. Even if you don't want it, even if you don't feel like you deserve it anymore, He is still reaching out and will continue doing so until the day you decide to let go of it all and take His hand. Why hold onto the bitterness and hatred another day? Make today the day you break down the barriers of pride and accept help, healing, and true peace and rest. God does for us what we cannot do for ourselves. He frees us from our bondage whatever it may be—pride, anger, you fill in the blank. No matter what your past has been, no matter what it has taken for you to get here, God tells you to look it square in the eye, unafraid, and watch Him work salvation and deliverance in your life. We don't have the power but He does, and our job is to simply keep our doubting and unbelieving mouths closed. There is story after story in the Bible of those whose faith in their weakness made them strong. Gideon, Barak, Samson, Jephthah, David, and Samuel are just a few of the great men that Hebrews 11:33-34 refers to: "By faith these people overthrew kingdoms, ruled with justice, and received what God had promised them. They shut the mouths of lions, quenched the flames of fire, and escaped death by the edge of the sword. Their weakness was turned to strength. They became strong in battle and put whole armies to flight" (NLT). This is a promise that God can, and will, rescue you wherever you are.

"For when I am weak, then I am strong" (2 Cor. 12:10 NLT). What an inspiring statement. The awesome, supernatural, miracle-creating power of God is available to us. Helplessness and weakness . . . I used to hate them but God loves them, and because of them God is able to use me. If we can just let go, we can have so much more. Much easier said than done, I am the first to admit. I am a work in progress.

Victory Comes through Surrender

Then Jesus said to His disciples, "If any of you wants to be my follower, you must turn from your selfish ways, take up your cross, and follow me. If you try to hang on to your life, you will lose it. But if you give up your life for my sake, you will save it."

—*Matthew 16:24-25 NLT*

The more we let God take us over, the more truly ourselves we become— because He made us. He invented all the different people that you and I were intended to be . . . It is when I turn to Christ, when I give up myself to His personality, that I first begin to have a real personality of my own.

—*C. S. Lewis*

The actual act of surrendering is the easiest thing you will ever have to do. Getting to the place where you are ready to surrender may, in fact, be the hardest. Mistrust, fear, and pride all get in the way of true surrender. You have been engaged in a battle; you have been laboring under the strain of what life has been throwing at you. But you have made it this far. You have survived your journey through the valley. You have quite possibly even looked death in the face and walked the other way. If, however, you have made it this far on your own, you know it is exhausting work. The burden you carry is great. Are you ready to claim victory through surrender? It sounds like an impossibility considering our widely accepted connotation of surrender. We are taught that victory and surrender are opposites: one side surrenders, and the other side claims the victory. But through Christ, they are one and the same, and the Lord has an invitation for you: "Come to me, all of you who are weary and carry heavy burdens, and I will give you rest" (Matt. 11:28 NLT). Stop laboring, stop battling, stop trying to do it on your own, and instead, claim victory over your hardships, trials, and hurts and experience true rest and peace.

God is waiting on *you* with open arms, with a love greater than we can comprehend. When you are tempted to doubt, remember this: "I have written *your* name on the palms of my hands" (Isa. 49:16 NLT, emphasis mine). God knows *you*; He knows the number of hairs on your head (Matt. 10:30 NLT). He knows your thoughts, dreams, desires, hurts, disappointments, and failures—and bigger than that, He gave His Son up, sacrificed Jesus' life in order to rescue you. I lost a child, and I cannot imagine willingly giving up my son's life for a complete stranger, a stranger who may or may not even accept the gift of that sacrificed life. "But God showed His great love for us by sending Christ to die for us while we were still sinners" (Rom. 5:8 NLT). If that isn't love, I don't know what is.

Because He loves you, He will never leave you. "This is my command—be strong and courageous! Do not be afraid or discouraged. For the Lord your God is with you wherever you go" (Josh. 1:9 NLT). Even when you refuse to acknowledge His presence, He is still there. Even when you turn your back on Him, He is still waiting. He will never give up on you. Do not interpret your numbness as His absence. "I am with you always, even to the end of the age" (Matt. 28:20 NLT).

"For I know the plans I have for you, says the Lord. They are plans for good and not for disaster, to give you a future and a hope" (Jer. 29:11 NLT). They are plans for good, even when you don't understand it and can't see it, that is God's promise. And when you have those days when you can't see the good, when you feel completely beaten down, surrender to God's power, as Paul encouraged: "I also pray that you will understand the incredible greatness of God's power for us who believe in Him. This is the same mighty power that raised Christ from the dead and seated Him in the place of honor at God's right hand in the heavenly realms" (Eph. 1:19-20 NLT). I assure you, the same God who raised Christ from the dead is able and waiting to take on whatever problems you can throw at Him.

A wounded heart that doesn't receive healing is an open door for sin. Through the suffering of Jesus, God has provided the healing for our hurts. Jesus Himself suffered all the hurts that one could suffer, and it is God's desire to heal our hurts but He must have control of our whole heart before He can heal it. God will only change that which He has control over. God looks upon us with grace and unfaltering, unconditional love, waiting for us. God wants us to turn to Him when we are hurting, so that He may be our comforter. He wants us to run to Him when we are frightened, so that He may be our protector. He wants to be our soft-place to fall.

Here is what this all boils down to. We must surrender all. If the Lord is God, follow Him. If you can trust Him for eternity, can't you trust Him for today?

So, how do you get there? How do you get to the place where you can trust God and let go of everything? How do you find love, joy, strength, the power to change the unchangeable? How do you find hope beyond helplessness, faith beyond fear, peace beyond bitterness? How can you begin to find beauty in the middle of the mess you find yourself in? Have you found yourself searching? The answer lies in the most beautiful mess of all.

The cross has become a universal Christian symbol. You can buy crosses in sterling silver, 14k gold, adorned with diamonds, rubies, beautiful gemstones. Jewelers make them into striking showpieces. But there was none of that beauty on the Roman cross on which Jesus was hung. This was the first-century equivalent of an electric chair or gas chamber. No death was more dreaded by criminals. None was as slow or painful or humiliating. It was so inhumane, Roman law did not permit a citizen of the empire to die by crucifixion. The cross, so shameful, so gruesome, so messy, has become the most beautiful symbol that we have ever looked upon. The influence of the cross has become the mightiest power in all of the world. The most horrible death imaginable for the Son of God became the price for our redemption. God took this horrifying mess and made it beautiful for us! The beauty of the cross has nothing to do with silver or gold or precious jewels. Its true beauty lies in the mess of the crucifixion, in the shame, in the separation that Jesus experienced when He took on the sins of the world, your sin and my sin. This beauty has everything to do with grace and mercy and forgiveness.

Surrender; wave the white flag. You won't be weakened; you aren't admitting defeat. Instead, you are taking hold of God's power and claiming victory! Give it to God; give it all to Him. He can handle it, your mess, your life—none of it is too big or small for God—and then get out of the way and watch Him work.

"And God will wipe away every tear from their eyes; there shall be no more death, not sorrow, not crying. There shall be no more pain, for the former things have passed" (Rev. 21:4 NKJV).

Scripture says, "For all have sinned and fall short of the glory of God" (Rom. 3:23 NIV) and "the wages of sin is death, but the gift of God is eternal life in Christ Jesus our Lord" (Rom. 6:23 NIV).

Jesus paid the price for us on the cross, and this precious gift of life, peace, and hope can be ours if we simply believe in Him. We don't need to do anything other than place our faith in Christ to accept this gift.

> But when the God our Savior revealed His kindness and love, He saved us, not because of the righteous things we had done, but because of His mercy. He washed away our sins, giving us a new birth and new life through Jesus Christ our Savior. Because of His grace He declared us righteous and gave us confidence that we will inherit eternal life. (Titus 3:4, 7 NLT)

> "For everyone who calls on the name of the Lord shall be saved" (Rom. 10:13 NLT).

Are you tired of feeling alone? Do you want to know peace, hope, and rest? Are you angry with God? Are you angry with yourself, with someone else? Are the what-ifs plaguing you and you feel like you're drowning in guilt? Does your heartache continue without reprieve until you feel like your heart is breaking into a million pieces? Do you want to know God? Do you know God and need to renew your relationship?

> Lord, You know what is on my heart today. Please help to heal my hurt and soften my loss. Help me to see You today,

Lord, in everything I do and say. Lord, I surrender my life to You, and though I may not understand why You have allowed this to happen, I know that You are in control. Forgive me, Lord, for questioning You. I trust You, Lord, and only You, and I accept your gift of forgiveness and salvation. Thank You for dying to save me. Amen.

It isn't magic. God may not change your situation, but He can change your heart . . .

All to Jesus, I surrender. All to Him, I freely give.

Through the valley . . . deep. *Through* the valley . . . dark. *Through* the valley . . . dreadful. But I am not alone, nor are you, so do not be afraid. By the grace of God, we *will* make it through.

CPSIA information can be obtained at www.ICGtesting.com
Printed in the USA
LVOW06s0000021013

354965LV00001B/4/P